Earth-blood

&

Star-shine

Cover Design: Sally Johnson

Thank you: Hannah Bissell, Teresa Mei Chuc, Adam Davis, Brian Schott, Humanities Montana, Montana Arts Council, Montana Conservation Corps

ISBN-13: 978-0-9915772-8-6 ISBN-10: 780991577286

Library of Congress Control Number: 2018933414

Shabda is the Sanskrit word for "sound, speech." Shabda is the sound current vibrating in all creation referred to as the Audible Life Stream, Inner Sound, and Word. Founded in June 2011 by Teresa Mei Chuc, Shabda Press' mission is to bring forth the luminous words and sounds of new, emerging, and established voices.

Published by Shabda Press Pasadena, CA 91107 www.shabdapress.com

Acknowledgments: Poems in this book were originally published in the following magazines and literary journals:

Adelaide Magazine, Antiphon, As It Happens, Barking Sycamores, Big Windows Review, Canary, Cape Rock, Cardinal Sins, Carnival, Chariton Review, Chicago Quarterly Review, Clover, Cobalt Review, Crack the Spine, Cutthroat, Drumlummon Views, Drunk Monkeys, Easy Street, Eretz Literary Review, Flathead Living, Front Range Review, Futures Trading, The Good Man Project, Harbinger Asylum, Hawaii Pacific Review, ICON, Iodine Poetry Review, Illuminations, Limestone, Main Street Rag, MO: Writings from the River, Naugatuk River Review, Pacific Review, Pilgrimage, Prick of the Spindle, Quail Bell Magazine, River Poets Journal, South Dakota Review, Spectrum, Quarry West, Whitefish Review, White Pelican Review, Verse Virtual, Visions International, Wilderness House Poetry Review, The Worcester Review, Yokoi.

Poems in this book also appeared in these anthologies:

Wilderness Walks (Montana Wilderness Association, 2017), *Bright Bones: Contemporary Montana Writing* (Open Country Press, 2018), *We Take Our Stand: Writers Protecting Public Lands* (edited by Rick Bass, 2017), *Adelaide Voices Literary Award Anthology* (Adelaide Books, 2018).

A previous version of "Waking Alone" won the Hollingsworth Prize from *White Pelican Magazine*.

Created, designed, and produced in the United States.
Printed in the United States.

Earth-blood

&

Star-shine

Poems by

Lowell Jaeger

Prolog: A Meditation

A Meditation

Two men in orange vests
hoist a roadkill doe
into a dump truck.

One man takes firm hold
of the forelegs, the other man
grasps the deer's hind legs awkwardly
at the ankles. Both swing the carcass
back and forth; at the count of three
let her fly and thunk into the truck bed . . .

I'm stopped in a line of traffic behind a flagger,
waiting for the pilot car to edge us safely
past smoldering miles of blackened lodgepole spires.
Long, hot months of dry-lightning wildfires
and ashen skies. The percussive *thuck thuck*
of Forest Service copter blades slapping
back the advancing blaze. Slurry bombers
rumbling back to basecamp for another fill-up and go.

And if I were a doe, I'd be driven — by the smell of char
and the fearsome noises — to flee, to wend
carefully down the mountainside
through the soft hush of what few pines remain,
to follow the dried creek bed
and stand hidden
where it crosses the highway.

Then dash, finally, from a thicket of alders
when desperation moved me
across two lanes of pavement . . .

and if all goes well, I'd lie down
in sight of the lakeshore, the water's blue
glittered lapping. Till under cover of moonlight,
I'd rise again, stand alert, step gingerly
into the shallows, wet my parched tongue
with long, cool swallows
of earth-blood and star-shine.

I. Earth

Forgive me, sweet earth, for not being shaken
out of the heavy sleep of self.

— Steve Kowit

Quick are the mouths of earth,
and quick the teeth that fed upon this loveliness.

— Thomas Wolfe

Wondrous World

Many wonders I've beheld in this wondrous world
of canyons and chasms and summits of sculpted snow.
None so radiant, so indelible, as my daughter,
nine years old, perched on a granite ledge, dangling her legs,
awash in sunshine above a slope of scree slanting
into an alpine meadow of riotous and frantic blooms.

I'd left her there while I scouted our most favorable
path of descent. And navigated to her side again
by the music of her song — a child's song she'd learned
for the pageant at school. Her bird-like voice in the breeze
amidst the incense of nectar. Her smile and rejoicing
wave upon my return. A dozen mountain goats,

curious, nosing closer, transfixed to witness
this ever-unfolding wondrous world. Where I,
like the goats, paused in reverence. And like the goats,
I inched forward toward her, while clouds above
continued to flow, and blossoms widened
to the sky's melodious allure. And beneath us

ancient strata rose toward daylight through dark.

The Muddy Banks of Little Rib River

Spied him belly-up in duckweed
and cattails, his gills green with pond scum.
I'd been wandering the shoreline, last days of summer
before school, casting for pike. And treble-hooked him,

snagged the old geezer, reeled him ashore
through putrid muck, a maze of lily pads,
as if he were no more than a drift-log.

My god, you're a mess, I said.
Like he didn't know it already.
Like he didn't guess I was going to say it
long before I said it.

What do you make of a god like that,
all stink and bloat? And beautiful
when the late-afternoon gilded August sun
shone rainbows in the slime. His spike

teeth glistening, his eyes so wide
the entire sky floated inside. His scales, a glittered mosaic,
an ancient design by which the frogs
and dragonflies silenced in awe.

I'd heard in school how god was dead.
Somebody famous and wise said that.
And here he was, not breathing, and breathed
as much as the water breathed each morn onward

through dark. And I walked home
emptyhanded, as the earth breezed on
— terrible and lovely — luscious mud
squirming between my bare toes.

Along the Trail to Hidden Meadow

A swallowtail perches on my blue bandana. Stays
with me as I catch my breath
in rippled shade of the aspens' quake.

Waits while I think back
to whole Julys without school,
swinging my long-handled net
through sunlit meadows hip-deep
in goldenrod, ragweed, yarrow.

I labored those summers to be proud
of the mounting board, my trophies
labeled rank and file, glittered scales
chalking my prints on the killing jar.

And couldn't shake a nagging shame
I'd robbed the meadow of its flutter.
Lepidoptera are sweet people.
Some say, holy.
                            This one
pauses in the aspens' whisper.
Fans his wings against my bandana

like no specimen under glass
knows how.

Tilt

I've lived a beaded cord of changing seasons,
and thank the tilted earth for that. Slant
sun drifting southward, cooling October's
red and gold, summer's dying embers
knee-deep for children kicking through them
on their walk to school.
                              Thrill of waking
to winter's first snowfall, knowing it's there
— window blinds closed — hearing new slush
on the road, wheels hushing along slowly, neighbors
lufting shovels of crystals curbside.
                              In April,
the birds' early morning playful incantations,
— joyous as I am — when blankets of white recede,
giving breath to meadow, courage to mule deer
browsing for nublets of green.
                              Along the lakeshore
today, I parked to marvel how jagged ice-fractures
buckle or widen when floes collide.
                              Spoke
with two boys lobbing melon-sized rocks, testing
how much weight our thinning crust of winter
might survive. Eager for June again. For diving headlong
into daredevil swimming holes, or rowing out
beyond the bay, trolling for spike-toothed pike.

Dinosaurs

My son and I edge our way up
steep sides of a badlands ravine.
We stare at scrabble, scanning for shards
of fossilized bone, searching for telltale
shades of dusty rust-orange hidden
in ancient grey ocean bottom rubble and scree.

We stare. And stare longer. He stoops
to gather another chunk of rib or chip of jaw,
and he can name the particular something-a-saurus
who — eons before us — foraged here
on tropical beaches now gone bone dry.

He's hefting a canvas pack of treasure, his eyes
like raptors' eyes, honed to razor focus.
I claim only a handful of what I suspect
could be worth holding onto, knowing I'm half-blind
in my ignorance and lack of practice.

My son, too, says he can cross the same ground
succeeding days and marvel at all he'd passed over —
layered mysteries, millions of years lost, now risen
transformed, invisible as we are to window seat passengers
jetting across the cloudless high blue. We don't exist

as far as they can see: a man and his son inching
up a difficult slope, obscured in a jumbled landscape.
While a parched wind murmurs through prairie grass.
While a meadowlark, hidden from view, trills and whistles.
Even the gods may never find us.

On the horizon, mountains collide, lifting
buried strata, inching skyward.

The Lion

While huffing my way up switchbacks
of a treeless rocky trail, I've sensed
the presence of something watching.
I've stopped, held still in the empty terrain,
looked up and down and around and saw

nothing. And mocked myself, the spinal
electricity of my imaginary fears.
Laughed aloud and whistled my way
onward, reasoning my good vision
would clarify all there is to reveal.

But I've been uncertain of my sight
since, some years back, my wife and I
visited a zoo. Stood in front of
the mountain lion's den. Pressed our faces
between the bars. And waited for the lion.

The lion who wasn't there. Who wasn't there
until he twitched his long tail as if
to wake us. As if he'd been a rock till now,
staring straight at us with the plainness
of a rock's eye, seeing all we see
                              and more.

Crossing Over

A steep climb, lots of strain, a pounding pulse . . .
and now the trail switches back and forth downhill
through alders and hellebore. And blackflies
buzzing my ears. Spring runoff
burbling in a verdant draw, yonder,

where I plan to bathe
sweat and salt from my shoulders and neck,
splash glacial melt on my sunburnt face.

When I arrive creek-side,
I'll need to ford and find where the footpath continues
somewhere yet unseen. I'll calculate
how to step stone-to-stone and keep dry.

And I'll err as always, failing
to read which exposed river rocks have anchored
themselves, or which will wobble and falter . . .

as I stumble and laugh aloud, landing knee-deep
in the sobering flow. The chill biting past my boot laces,
soaking socks and blisters, waking in me
an ancient joy: to gasp a last lungful of daylight,
my heart
jolted, my chest aflame
with the radiance of creation,
and the wide, resplendent sky.

Back Away, Slowly

A radio news report:
bears invading the suburbs,
foraging for dumpster pizza crusts
instead of wild berries and nuts.

A few neighborhoods brazenly
bait the hairy beasts with table scraps,
snap photos, blog to friends. One
especially enlightened housewife
has evolved to where she swears
she longs to embrace Ursus Americanus
eye-to-eye and read his "soul."

I'm only listening sidewise
as I drive, and shiver a bit
to imagine Cindy Cul-de-Sac
fluttering her eyelids
at the tall dark stranger
who's ripped apart the bird feeders,
shredded her garbage for morsels of steak.

A bear's nose provides
a window to his soul, if
he's got one. He's seduced
by a putrid carcass bloated with rot, abuzz with flies.

He's no sentimentalist.
He's no lover of surprise.

Possession/Obsession

Someone has set a crib in the gravel
beside the dumpster. A wooden crib,
festooned with stenciled teddy bears,
pink and blue, three out of four
roller wheels still intact, varnished
rails chipped — maybe chewed —
though all in all it's in useable shape,
free for the taking should a needy family
happen by to happily haul it home.

Someone else has set out a plastic crate
of assorted women's purses, several of which
still have sale tags attached. And someone else
has stacked four truck tires, well-worn
but good enough, maybe, for an ambitious
high-schooler's shop project.
Beside the tires, a chest of drawers,
and beside the chest of drawers, a monster
TV, no doubt a real splurge when it was new.

It's true — isn't it? — there's no clear marker
as to what's trash and what's not. Difficult
to distinguish what to part with and when.
Such agony. And meanwhile a mini-van . . .
mom, dad, three sleepy-eyed boys, and a beagle.
Mom hefts two sacks of aluminum cans.
Put 'em over there, Dad says, pointing

toward the crib, the purses, the tires,
the chest of drawers, and the TV. *They're worth
a buck or two for scrap.* The boys uncover
a castoff set of golf clubs in the weeds.
Leave it, Dad says, but the boys ignore him.
The beagle noses everything. Mom drapes
one of the purses over her shoulder
as if it belonged to her all along.

Don't Be Obscene

Like shoving your arm
up a cow's vagina, says
the freckle-faced ranch kid.

Don't be obscene! says
his teacher.

I'm today's classroom guest.
We'd been discussing
our country's quagmire wars
in foreign lands.
Our brothers, fathers, sons
in uniform.

You go in hoping you'll
save the calf, says the kid.
You're only guessing, groping
for what's wrong and how
to set it right.

Don't be obscene!
his teacher insists, sternly.
She's worried I'll be offended
by the kid's unexpected metaphor.

Deeper than your elbow, says
the kid, *before you know it.*
Kinda stuck for what comes next.
Now there ain't no quick exit.
Now there's gonna be pain.

Life on Mars

News interview with a space program boss:
He contends humanity must push to colonize
Mars. In case we need to abandon this planet,
he says, Mars is our most likely new residence.

Then, news of wars flaring up
in hotspots across the globe. Rumors
of escalating armaments, threats of attack.
News about kids killing kids in school.
News about building a big wall at the border.
News about contaminated drinking water.
All the usual, I thought. All the usual . . .

and caught myself drifting from listening,
trying to picture the citizens of this rock migrating
to the next rock over. What to bring? What to cast
aside? Like packing up the old homestead and unloading
down the road. On a significantly grander scale.

And recalled helping my neighbor dolly appliances
out the door and into his rented van. Boxes
of dishes, pots, and pans. Hampers of linens. He and his wife
crabbing at each other over what goes where.
Their progeny throwing clods in the driveway
till one ran crying because the others had bloodied his nose.

We hefted basement couches into the daylight. Lifted
cushions to check for cockroaches, but
couldn't be sure. All of us enthused
at the prospect of a new locale. Shook down
a nest of spiders from a set of box springs. Worried
there were eggs in there, too, but couldn't reach them. Witnessed
a stowaway mouse scurry aboard from under the stove.

What the Guidebook Says and Doesn't Say

The guidebook warned us about "scammers,"
but what they were, or how we should identify
who they were, wasn't explained. So
we took to the streets in Rome, alone
with our lack of understanding. Ventured
up one picturesque lane lined with shops
and down another. Saw what we'd expected

and missed the rest. Tired ourselves out
and stood numb at an anonymous intersection,
thinking we'd better find food to refuel
our flagging instincts. Musing how life is much the same
one side of the globe or the next. One gets
tired and hungry and turns with nostalgia toward home.
This is, of course, when surprise happens, when

out of nowhere, as if they'd been beside us all along,
an elderly woman and a young girl came burbling
in our faces with a spray of foreign speech,
the old one wanting to show us the young one's baby,
that much we could guess. No sooner did we smile
our miscomprehension than lickity split that piss-wet
infant I'd cradled to my chest, my wife and I

cooing and gushing politely, thinking the guidebook
never intimated how swiftly locals might love us
like instant kin. And just as swiftly
they were gone, around the corner, out of sight.
Well, we still needed food, didn't we? Who can resist
Italian cuisine? And how does one explain to the waiter
when he delivers the bill, somewhere you've lost

your wallet. And camera. Your thoughts reel back
to that amazingly friendly old crone, how
when she filled your arms with her grandchild,
she'd sidled close with her shoulders and thighs
and run her hand up and down your back, leaving you
with this: a reminiscence wide as the Colosseum,
ruined as the ruins, outlasting all the photos never taken.

Bread and Meat and Cheese

As a tourist, I yearn to ramble
cobbles worn through history
to a visible groove, pathways
carved by mules and carts.

I want to stand in a 500-year-old plaza
and read names on the plaques of statuary
— architects, warriors, princes, and poets —
then lift my gaze to nearby highrise
citadels of glass and chrome glinting
under the persistent sun, as if to promise
an end to the age of suffering and injustice.

I don't want these beggar children,
smudge-faced runny-nosed reminders
of lasting desperation. Hands
adjuring from shadowed doorways.
Or packs of disconsolate voices, whining
and buzzing at my ears like stinging gnats.

The front-desk attendant advises: *As long
as you provide them with coins,
their meth-addicted parents
will send them out collecting.* He looks away
and adds: *Imagine what happens
if they return home empty-handed.*

You look hungry, I say to a beggar-child.
I am, she replies. When I offer her bread
and meat and cheese, she refuses.
Her eyes are the eyes of a mad dog.
She stares at the food. Impossible

to name her sadness.
It's so much bigger than that.

Montana Highway

This wide expanse of highway divides
miles of densely forested wilderness.
An uplifting drive, solitary, and both sides of the road
appear to be yours because no one else
is there. Always a temptation — straightaways
through dappled sunlight and strobing
shadows of tall pines — to punch the accelerator
and let your speed climb.

      Ah, but crowds inhabit
here, unseen. A metropolis of deer and elk.
An occasional moose will emerge from brambles,
forsaking camouflage long enough to dash across
the asphalt chasm.

Friend, sooner or later, each of us will know our station.
Our bones, glistening with star-shine in the ditch,
will molder and decay.

This enchanting day, an open road. Thrill of speeding
one place to another. Overhead — beyond our vision —
calamitous fragments
of creation go racing headlong, orbiting what seems
like endless space.

     Until surprise comes crashing.

Wonderment

Well, we nearly died, but so what? The runaway
truck came charging our car broadside, surely
would have smashed us, crushed us, ground our bones
to little more than a grease spot on the concrete byway.

Within hours, whatever couldn't be collected and towed,
the cleanup crews would hose into roadside shards
and brambles. Traffic would resume whooshing past,
rolling over the ghost of us. The sun would set, the moon rise.

The point is this: It could have happened but did not.
No one typed our names in the obits next evening.
No one delayed comfortable routine to mourn. No one
could hold to anyone and decry our tragic demise.

Afterward you pulled to the shoulder, shaken and pale,
kneeled in the ditch and vomited.
I couldn't muster common sense enough
to offer you a wet rag, couldn't

erase the imprint of that truck driver's wide-eyed panic
as he clamped his boot to the brake pedal
and downshifted,
quaking haplessly at the mercy
of an ordinary morning
teetering
on the jagged edge of lasting regret.

Chores: Milking

Each of the heavy barn doors had to be lifted
on its hinges to drag it closed, for which the boy
bunched his shoulders, huffed, and struggled.
While inside the dim, Dolly waited in her stanchion,
breathing slow, her puffs of steam rising past the hayloft
through shafts of moonlight, dust-laden air
roiling in the beams.

The boy froze with bucket and stool in hand — listened
to the night's howl, the creaking rafters. Listened
to his heart's muffled drumbeat, its persistent thrum.

In a flash, the boy's daydreaming soul
lifted through the roof's loosened shingles
to a mind's-eye view of the farm, its little farmhouse,
windows lit and flickering. Mother, Father, brothers, sister . . .
each of them sailing lonely in the sweeping black emptiness
of the same small rooms.

        Till the boy felt like a far-off star staring
down, aching and afraid for something he couldn't name.

And suddenly he was glad to have chores. Awakened
where he'd landed again inside his shoes, sheltered
in the familiar barn, smells of manure and straw, bucket and stool

still in hand, and Dolly fidgeting with anticipation.

A Bit Bewildered

I stop, breathless. Kneel at the creek.
I'm lost. Eat a sandwich. Take a leak.
Catalog the contents of my pack. Knife,
matches, flashlight. Jerky to save my life

a day or two. Should be panicked but I'm not.
Think back where I've been. How I got
where I am. Twisted luck. Surprise
outcomes. Wrong turns, logic-wise,

brought me places I never dreamed I'd go.
Like here. The sun sparkles in the water's flow.
Ancient rocks. Meadow. Sedges and flowers.
I've got sturdy boots. Daylight for hours.

I follow the game trail as it climbs toward views.
Imagine my obit in next week's news.

Waking Alone

I wake alone in the cold glare
of a full moon, ghostly shadows of tall pines cast
on bedroom walls, dancing. Clatter
of hooves on rock in the corral
uphill behind the house. Two mares,

sleepless as watchdogs on a night like this.
Unseen trouble in the brambles
and bushes, rustling. I've stopped
turning by instinct across the blankets
to an emptiness beside me. I know it's there.
Listen to the horses . . . snort, stomp,

snap at each other like bickering sisters.
Pull on my jeans and boots, walk out
to calm them. Or is it to dampen the clamor
in my own head, the mad stallion
of desire?
                    Skye and Autumn stretch their necks
across the rails to greet me. I palm
the soft upper lip and doeskin just above,
read the flicker and pulse of each nostril's quiver.

Shadows dart, tree to tree. Rocks
slide somewhere nearby and the earth
trembles. Both horses whinny and pace
the fence line. The moon floats alone through space.
Each star consumed with its own burning.
I shiver and whisper to the mares.

Omens

Seems like it should mean something,
we say. Outside our classroom windows
a squadron of black-jacketed grackles
had lifted in a frenzied gyre to battle
an interloping magpie. Amidst the fray
half a dozen birds spun from their orbits
to crash against the glass; no casualties tallied
beyond a handful of feathers, unhinged.

We're left a bit spooked, breathless, grasping
for an explanation, weaving into service
our powers of reason to mark this day
with dark intent, an old crone rising within us,
connecting the stars to build a story.

Birds quarrel, flurry, and fly. We recount
the inexplicable with far-off gazes, wizened
and beaming. We can read the signs. *Something*
will surely happen, we say. We're certain of it.

And something always does.

An Awakening

It's quiet as death. Till a renegade wolf in the dark
scents his prey. Dances under star-shine and howls
a quarter mile away. Chills the forest
a blacker black. You blink. Listen. Stare.
The pulse of your empty house skips a beat.
In the barn, the horses nicker and kick.

The mare, ready to foal, paces sick
with fear — panting and soaked in sweat.
You lace your boots and snipe out where
watching eyes of trees have guessed
your savage intention: hunt whatever prowls
with teeth, claws, or Satan's bark.

Just beyond the fence line you find the track.
Yours are acres the wild wants back.

II. Blood

The incredible death-work
that is the life of the universe.

— Stephen Dunn

A Wayside in History

Plaque tacked next to the mount on the wall
at a backroad wayside in Iowa . . . says,
last moose sighted nineteen something or other
by farmer so and so, who rose one fateful morn
and spotted the beast trampling and bumbling his way
through acres of corn.

                  O, farmer, land-husband
— he who hath been entrusted
with dominion over creatures great and small,
he who once was lost in the wilderness himself,
he who wants tomorrow wide and wonderful
for his grandchildren, he who scratches to survive
sunrise to sunset on a wobbly remnant of star-slag
in the dead center of nowhere, he who

                          in sleepless hours
considers the cosmic odds against him, the odds
against us all, the odds against undoing
what's been done —

                such a ruthless
pack of savages we are when confronted
with a once-in-a-lifetime miracle;
we load our big guns, chase the stranger down,
and drop him in the cow pasture, heavy
as the sad fly-buzzing carcass of a beached whale.

Suspense

A ramped walkway lowers slowly
from the burnished silver spacecraft . . .
while townsfolk watch at the edge
of a cornfield, children halfway hide
behind mothers' aprons, farmers in coveralls
brandish pitchforks. Everyone braced
to meet the creature from beyond.

It's an old TV movie, an imprinted chill
down my childhood spine as the alien reveals himself,
his almost human form. Except he's naked,
bald, somewhat reptilian, apparently unarmed,
maybe harmless, though we're gasping
and disgusted to encounter a stranger

so strange. I was innocent enough not
to guess we'd murder him straight away.
And later we'd learn he'd intended to rid humanity
of pestilence and famine. Tragedy puzzled me
back then, not now. It's like this: One of us snaps
a flash photo; the star-man stumbles, blinded . . . and he lurches
toward us.
          Then a shotgun drops him.

MAN BAGS TWO TROPHIES WITH ONE SHOT

My mother clipped her local news and mailed to me
a story about two young bucks during rutting season
who'd quarreled and locked horns. Battled
till one lost all, possibly to starvation,
having so inextricably attached himself
to the other's rage.
                              The victor,
stumbled some time later
under the crosshairs of the rifle's scope,
and the surprised hunter reported sighting the deer
"waltzing erratically"
sideways and backwards through a thicket
of alders and hackberries. Wondrous
as that might sound, he pulled the trigger
even so.

The state biologist estimated
the buck who died with a slug in his heart
had lugged the "badly decomposed carcass"
of his foe for nearly six moons,
possibly over forty miles of mountainside.
Said coyotes likely fed on the dead flesh
at night — only the spine, forelegs, and head remained —
and had pursued the buck to the end
of his grisly ordeal.
                              Now I read
and carry new burden on my brow.
I wonder what prompted my mother
in aiming this account at me. I wonder
if the hunter draws any lesson here.
I've forgotten the exact numbers,
but someone tallied the points on each rack.

Voodoo Mood

Three of us manned steaks on the grill,
boozy and a bit melancholy as late afternoon
clouds of gunmetal-blue roiled our horizon.

Through patio glass, we could hear the wives
clinking dinnerware, forks and spoons and knives,
their laughter boiling up from easy chatter.

We had almost nothing to say, us three, till
a voodoo mood covered the sun, chilled us
to whisper, shoulder to shoulder, youthful memories

of birds and beasts we'd shot just for the hell of it,
just for the suffering and gore. One said
he'd lie prone beside a boulder, wait for prairie dogs

and plink them dead, one by one, as they rose
to sample daylight. Hundreds, he said. He'd swing 'em
by the tail, sling 'em into the weeds. Walk home

and never look back. The other grinned and said
he'd scatter-gunned dozens of magpies he'd baited
in a wire cage. And I said . . . well . . .

I don't want to say what I said, and I'm sorry
I said it. Each of us, older now, cringed to know
how limited the pleasures our cruelties had won.

And as we sat beside our vivacious wives
— each exclaiming how tender the meat on her plate —
we chewed and chewed. And struggled to swallow.

Same Story: She Tells It or He Tells It

Back home from the Department of Natural
Resources and Obstetrics, where I'd succeeded in line
for a deer tag and a pregnancy test,
I canceled calendar weeks backwards
to my last period and counted forward to the opening
day of hunting season, my biological clock
tocking with a bad case of buck fever.

Cleaned and oiled my rifle, twice. Hung
Winnie-the-Pooh curtains in the spare bedroom.
Splotched the walls with forest green
camo. Bought a crib, bassinet,
and re-loading kit. A GPS locator,
and a book of baby names. All
duct-taped in a diaper bag, ready to roll.

At sunrise, I slipped into my long-johns
and wool socks. Bundled a decent robe
and new pair of fuzzy slippers. Grabbed
an orange ammo vest. Threw a six-pack
in the cooler, couple of Spam sandwiches,
and my prenatal vitamins. Then . . .
vomited, a bit hungover from the night before.

Actually, I'd been nauseous every morning for weeks,
and confess — with my head in the toilet —
I questioned whether I had nerve enough
to withstand hunting full-term. But the truck was loaded,
my breasts were swollen . . . and my buddies
would never forgive me if I backed out now.

My god, bumping along for nine months
up and down those rutted logging roads
felt like something was kicking my guts out!
Hours and hours I bided my time
reading topo maps and *Mommy To Be.*
Nothing to shoot. Not a single contraction.

In the end it all happened so fast.
We'd parked the truck, determined
to flush what we could on foot, when my water broke,
and only a few Lamaze huffs up the trail,
the doctor exclaimed, *There it is!*
The head had crested. I centered the crosshairs
on the biggest, cutest buck
I'd ever dreamed . . . spread my legs wide,
and tried to remember how to squeeze
the trigger to make this one shot count.

Then BLAM! Felt like I'd split
in two. And there it lay, struggling to find
its breath, as I tallied points on the rack. Ten fingers, ten toes.
My baby! My baby! I shouted and rushed through the trees
till I cradled its warm flesh in my arms.
Then dragged it to the truck, drove home
to introduce my world to this beautiful creature
in the nursery
where I mounted its head on the wall.

Chainsaw Lament

My sister's pious stepson visits and stays
one morning too long. Over breakfast,
I snipe at his Christian College's
easy answers — *because the Bible says so.*
He's calm. My pulse quickens,
sharpens to whittle him down. Till
his shoulders cave, eyes go blank.

With my chainsaw's ragged-throat rage,
an hour later I'm dropping dead wood
for the small thrill to see it fall. And spy
a venerable buckskin larch, particularly thick
and reaching above the others. Irresistible.

I launch in, my saw's bar too short
to make this graceful. Bark so massive
it takes a bucket of sweat to chisel into the giant's
woody core. Till it moans and topples.

I shut the engine. Deathly quiet,
but for my heartbeat's drum. I'd cut him
to the ground. Not just his simple faith. Not
the slump in his spine as he left
the room. Something bigger.

Beetles file out from bore holes in the stump.
Stagger in daylight. Crushed juneberry branches
still in bloom, twitch and sway. I watch
small leaves on the forest floor watching me.

All of us uncertain what's to come.

Mr. Nasty

The clerk has refused him, politely.
So he's demanded to see the boss.

The boss concurs with the clerk
— no tags, no receipt . . . no refund —

So, he's demanded to see the boss's boss.
Now the clerk, the boss, and the boss's boss

stand stoic, stand firm, listening to Mr. Nasty
growl his red-faced threats and maledictions.

The clerk, the boss, and the boss's boss
monitor Mr. Nasty's bombast for worrisome signs

of what he might decide to do. Till
he marches off, muttering, kicking

at the automatic glass doors opening too slowly
to suit his rage . . . and then it's over.

He's gone. Among the survivors, I'm next in line.
We nod and whisper, aisles one through twenty-five,

working our way back toward smiles.
Even the concrete floor breathes a deep sigh.

Note to an Earlier Self

For a semblance of resolve, let's run the reel back
to that late afternoon on a graveled farm road
through monotonous miles of corn and soy,
an August sun sizzling your shoulders and thighs,
as you pedaled across the heartland, alone,
the longest year of your life,
waiting for a court date, waiting for papers to sign.

A rolling emptiness rose grudgingly, here to nowhere,
after crossing a bridge, wooden and decayed,
remember? In the muck below, a muskrat struggled
with a cable-snare, thrashing. Another nearby, slick
with scum, also ensnared, but this one lifeless,
drowned.
　　　　　It's like the click of shutter — isn't it? —
the way a simple glance can lodge in the brain,
while so much goes by we let pass . . . as if
behind our eyelids there's no one there.

And there she was, one hand raised head-high,
standing on the front porch of a weathered farmstead.
Truly, she was there, in the flesh, wasn't she? The bib
and skirt of her apron stained crimson. Tomatoes, maybe.
Or blood? You, with only a toehold on the cliffs of what's real,
did you invent this apparition? You waved. You saw blood,
and you kept going, muscling your way blindly forward,
immersed in vapors of guilt and ghosts of worn apprehensions.

Was her hand uplifted
for sake of shielding her eyes from the sun's lowering horizon?
Or was she beckoning to you, and you ignored her call?

Leavenworth

One extraordinary day you wake to rise
under a full moon and drive past sunup
a monotonous Interstate stone slab,
into an apprehensive flat expanse of Kansas,
miles of dusty heat-sopped shimmering haze.

Three no-nonsense badges in dark glasses
at the first gate. One standing statue-like
with a shotgun, watching. Another quizzing you
— your intentions, your I.D. and passcode —
while the other circles the car, peering
in the windows, catching your face following him

in the rearview mirror. Like being swallowed
when the first gate opens to the second gate,
and both lock shut behind you. Like swimming
in the belly of a whale, standing in line
at Reception, treading a whirlpool
of paperwork and permissions.
                                    The waiting room
drowning in worriment and dread,
brothers and wives and buddies who'd promised
to visit . . . and here we are. This once. At least
you can leave this place justified with that.
And you will drive home wide-eyed that evening
to the opulence of freedoms you call your own.

While the man you've come to see greets you
forever stone-faced, embarrassed maybe,
concealing the trials of his routine "inside."
The pair of you trading stares through reinforced glass,
shouting in the din of so many miseries. Groping
for pleasantries. Discovering none.

Understanding Numbers

Pulsing red lights, blue lights.
Cop-cars. An ambulance.
White sedan upside down
amidst a glitter of shattered glass.

I'm slowed in the opposite lane, almost
stopped cold, though a state patrolman
signals us to keep nosing onward, vehicle by vehicle,
inching past blood stains, flares, and caution cones.

All year long, I've survived this highway,
my daily commute, sailing heedlessly past
the obvious warning: an electronic billboard
tallying, week by week, state-wide traffic fatalities.

In March, 38. After July holidays, the reckoning
surged to 97. September now, 164.
Numbers. Only numbers, as if a faceless someone
mumbled a count while stringing pearls.

Until today, when I witnessed emergency crews
straining with a pry-bar to free the body
belted in the wreck. More than a number . . .
for the driver's wife restrained by paramedics,

her panicked eyes flashing red lights and blue,
as she labored — wiping crimson blotches from her sleeve —
where she stood unsteady beside the road, moaning
an anguished, *No, no. No, please, no.*

Consequences

He'd dropped his coat in the barn. His new
school coat, and Grandma said he mustn't fetch it back.
He mustn't run back in there, she said,
even to rescue what's survived
of Custer's platoon, or Sitting Bull's tribe.
And she tucked him closer, holding him
from dashing out and doing what he mustn't do.

While the panicked men frenzied
with hoses and buckets and shovels, in and out
the big barn door billowing smoke.
Soot-blackened faces, coughing spit, shouting
Get a move on it, Man! Quick!

His gut hurt, hearing Grandma murmur the word *consequences.*
Consequences this, consequences that.
Hurt, hearing the sad-eyed cows, newly homeless,
bunched at the fence line, bawling.
He worried Grandpa would forbid plans to rebuild
Fort Hay Bale. Couldn't answer Grandma, as to why Custer

set the little straw tepee aflame. And who
gave him the matches in the first place?
One blazing tepee led to three, then four, then more.
Whatever their ancient quarrel, he'd forgotten.
And still they'd insisted to battle with arrows
and cannons and war clubs. Couldn't make peace,
even if it cost them their own pretend skins
and their molded plastic scalps.

A Traveler's Tale

My son and I bumped along
a narrow jungle byway.
We stopped to enjoy a gang
of grey monkeys who swung
down from the branches
and climbed on our car, peering
in — as curious of us as we were

of them. Our hands, oversized
versions of theirs. Our eyes
reading their eyes. Till an old
native woman walked over
and the monkeys backed off,
sat quiet on the roadside.
Be careful, she said. *They bite.*

She threw a fistful of gravel —
the monkeys screamed
like animals. Like animals
they snarled and snapped
long sharp incisors,
blood red gums. Not at all
creatures we'd imagined they should be.

My son and I watched the woman
ambling back from where she'd come.
The monkeys watched us, sidewise,
inching closer. We rolled
the windows tight. The gang's
hairy little fingers evolving,
grasping toward lead pipes and knives.

The Nature Lesson

Beneath flickering grow lamps, early April,
in ranks of readied flats . . .
sprouts awakened, little fists of green pushing
up from soil, climbing toward light.

Then, too, a surprising lot of seeds failed,
lacking spark to burst forth, root, and rise.
Even seemingly healthy nublets
withered mysteriously, succumbed to root rot,
collapsed into puddles of verdant mush.

Transplanting time, mid-May, bedraggled seedlings
drooped, then toppled, as if sickened by overwhelming stress
of dislocation. Too much sunlight. Or too much shade.
Too wet. Too dry. Too sandy. Too much clay.
The loam too rich with nutrients, or the earth exhausted.

Bugs chewed wide leaves, leaving sculpted lace.
Grubs nibbled roots to useless nubs.
Late summer high noon, runners of zucchini scorched and wilted.
During starlit hours — deer, mice, and rabbits
raided and wrecked, munched and pillaged.

As best we knew, we nursed and repaired
the salvage, culling the least-most-fit
by jerking stalks from dirt and abandoning them
to heaps of compost. Wielded an arsenal of sprays
to combat mites, mold, blight and disease.

Less than bountiful, our harvest — buckets of beets, potatoes,
beans, one fat squash. So many start, so few survive.
Your hand touched mine as we twisted tomatoes from the vine.
All these years we've lasted. Struggled, and flourished.
The whole scheme of life, so dangerous, so strange.

Squirrels

One summer, God knows why, squirrels
multiplied to plague us. Squirrels darting like rats
into and out of the woodpile — impossible
to calculate an accurate census since they all look
pretty much the same. An army of squirrels commandeering
the crawlspace beneath our rooms. We heard them

chewing and chittering in the floor joists while we paused
on the sofa with our dinner trays downstairs, watching TV.
Squirrels gnawing and loosening pinecones, dropping them
— heavy as hardballs — banging on the barn's tin roof
earlier even than the robins burst forth raucously
with simpleminded songs of praise and wonder. Whole afternoons

we surveilled a squirrel team of demolition experts escaping
to their bunkers in the brambles beyond our lawn,
their jowls stuffed with cotton-candy muffs
of pink fiberglass insulation they'd salvaged
from inside our bedroom walls. Badass squirrels

who commenced with alarming boldness to chide us
if we dare walk too near their frenzied burglaries, scolding us
for not signing over the deed and surrendering
to accommodate their escalating appetites,
our dog and cats mewling plaintively, impounded,
lunging at porch screens as squirrels preened and teased them.

Lo, these were a breed of cocksure squirrels, so at home
with their providence they began to parade in the roses
with the pageantry of Caesar's legions. As if
there were no stopping them. As if
they'd forgotten the hardships of generations previous
and less fortunate.

As if they could ignore the shadows of hawks and ospreys
patrolling the open meadow. And, not long before
October's first cruel frost, the entire tribe
had vanished. As if it were perfectly natural.
As if, God only knows, it all transpired to proffer us
something to witness, something to think about.

The Woodrat

Splayed snout-first to the concrete floor
inside the toolshed's gloom
beneath the workbench . . .
the little grey woodrat.

Must have gnawed his way in
out of the snow and cold,
half-starved, half-blinded
driven by blood instinct
to survive and multiply.

Penny-sized puddle
of vomited ooze,
his last gasp after nibbling
pellets of strychnine.

I, executioner, scoop him
in a garden trowel, pause
to examine what remains . . .
fine translucent whiskers,
bead-like nose, front claws
distended, as if still grasping

the hollow victory of another day's
sustenance, the stinging irony
in struggling with soldier-like gallantry
smack into the arms
of his advancing demise.

Griz

Narrow trail twists through neck-high thickets
of alders and hellebore, climbs onward around a blind turn,
and there he is: big hunk of shaggy brown griz, stopped
in his tracks, nose in the air, sniffing
intruders' sweat wafting suddenly too near.

Three of us and one of him, sufficient heft on his bones
to bulldoze forward if he chooses, mulling this over
as he rocks on his forelegs, his hulking shoulders
flexing side to side.
                    Nothing to rescue us but precious little
time, as we step back, slowly, the way we came,
averting eye contact, even sidewise. Savvy enough
not to shuffle wrong and stumble. Outcome
could be blood, mostly our own.

And now he's looming above us, continuing past, as we
wait meekly, downhill side, scant yards off-trail.
He's god of where he wants to go. Our silence
is a kind of weak-kneed prayer.

The Pace of Change

Why does Brother Turtle bother
to cross the road when the other side
calls his blood to crawl forward?

The goal, in his low range of vision,
can't be more alluring than a green haze, the span
from here to there, from now till tomorrow,
from dream to accomplished fact.

He's clawed past the centerline, under
the hot spotlight of noonday sun, trembling
in the rumble of oncoming traffic.

Like falling cosmic junk or an out-of-nowhere
asteroid pounding downward,
Brother Turtle, that dump truck
heaped with rocks and gravel, charges toward us.

The driver, if there is one,
smokes a cigarette, drinks his java.
How swift the outcome.
Could be one way. Could be another.
In less than a gasp, he's gone by.

Miserable Wind

Miserable wind blasting the canvas tent
broadside, jolting us awake, wide-eyed;

my wife and I camped amidst the wretchedness
of tribes described in historical roadside

memorials — as if the wounded still languished
in the sage, as if pox-afflicted lodges still flamed,

the sky's tumultuous voices forever wailing. She and I
lift the comforter aside, crawl

past the tent flaps. We stand unprotected, in rags,
reeling in the dizziness of exhaustion, moonlit

cliffs of the great divide raging with vapors
quickened from flesh in the frigid night air,

stars flaring their rifle shots in the black,
the tempest bugling and charging toward us

where we lean together, shivering and small.

III. Star

I have one small drop of knowing in my soul.
Let it dissolve in your ocean.

— Rumi

Invisible

Last night, snow swathed the meadow.
This morning we scroll the window shades
and trace nature's busy history of trails,
hooves and clawed footfalls crisscrossing
acres blanketed white.

Such complicated comings and goings,
traversing so nearby
while we slumbered unsuspectingly.
Deer, elk, rabbit, squirrel, raccoon,
milling about the moonless overcast midnight.

Even now, invisible birds converse
in the treetops. Beneath winter's crust
an army of voles tunnels and toils
to construct a maze of hidden causeways.
Among beasts, we are bold and obvious and blind.

Beatiful winter mornings

alot of people think don't about animals

always See tracks in the snow every morning. and you hardly ever notice them

Hunting in the night dark in Sweden no clue of what animals know that im here.

after a while you loose track of beaulitul things in your every day life

Lost

The butt of her rifle recoiled painfully against her
collar bone. Slivered grains on the stock
scraped her chin. Still the shot tore true,
lofting shreds of buck flesh — as he sprang
over barbed wire — till the slug
in his chest dropped him to flounder
breathless in the cold blue late afternoon.

Next night she's recounting the hunt. Thawing
by my fire. She'd unaccountably
lifted her gaze skyward by half
a heartbeat, and the stag was up
and gone. In new snow, the blood trail
spilled through stands of hemlock.
Print for print up into the canyon,
she'd pursued his collapse, deeper
under tall pine, leap for leap.

Her fingers laced around a coffee cup,
she tells how she'd lost him
in the creek bed where one last footfall
on crushed watercress foretold nothing
more. How she'd turned slow circles,
mute, panting. How darkness gathered,
and boughs of hemlock hushed closed.

Sadness

Paint-chipped yellow rented rowboat. Eight-year-old
stepson and I afloat on murky waters one merciless
early morning, mosquitoes and blackflies
feasting on our necks and earlobes, humid doldrums
hazing a bake-oven sun. Few nibbles and no fish.
And no conversation. A man can outlive some sadness

but this memory wakes me at four a.m. and hounds me
hapless till dawn. How he never once dared complain,
even as we chewed our way through cheerless
sack-lunch snacks, even as we gulped warm cola
and nearly gagged. I'd flubbed it between us
long ago, but skip — for now — the blame for that.

Say I was untutored, lacked insight, deaf
to doubts about fatherhood in the first place,
his mother and I so locked in our own distractions
we mostly forgot the kid was there. No recollection
how I'd dozed off. Then woke in the bow of that boat,
bug-bitten, ashamed, and irritable. This outing . . .

we might have rowed together toward better memories
than we'd made till then. An hour
I'd been sleeping. And there he sat, staring
at a joyless puddle of bilge, too timid to speak,
his line tangled on hidden snags,
our boat drifting too shallow.

Strong Swimmer

Has to do with bone density, I'm told. Some people
float, others must labor hyper-passionately
to keep from going under. I'm mostly treading water,
striding from here to there, outwardly confident,
as if my destination is always near, while truly
I'm awash in riptides, gasping for air. That's me,

thrashing in the shallows for summers on end
before I managed a strategy to look like swimming.
Me, in the lifeguard chair, high school senior, donning
a strong-swimmer disguise. Me, a sinker,
slapping the waves frantically, panicked
I couldn't rescue myself from drowning.

How many of us are layered like that?
Zorro, for instance, swashbuckling as a Musketeer,
gallops into the Comandante's hacienda,
slashing with his sword as if it were a fountain pen,
his stylish signature "Z." Let's agree
there's a Zorro in each of us, pretending.

Who could have mistaken this hero's costume
as anything less than an exterior emblem
of the man's interior prevailing disconnections?
We are strange to others and stranger to ourselves.
Q. Who was that masked man?
A. With or without a mask, not an easy guy to get to know.

A Portrait

Ambled walkways and boulevards
beside the slow-flowing Seine. Watched
strangers passing. Didn't speak
the language, was bashful,
wore my collar up, shoulders hunched.
Blind with painted-on angst . . .
as a youth, I rumbled around like that.

Your portrait, no? she said, her easel apart
from a cluster of hucksters near Pont des Arts,
bridge of romance, bridge of sighs.
For you, mon cher, no money, she laughed.
I'd almost turned and sped away.
She had (who knows?) nothing better
pressing. And scraped at her drawing, feverishly,
smudging charcoal with her opened palm.

Mused this morning, years later, at my face
in the bathroom mirror. Such good times
I've missed out on. The people I might have known.
While I walked the streets, hands fisted
in my jacket pockets around an inexplicable emptiness
I couldn't grab onto and wouldn't let go.

She tore my portrait from her pad
when she'd concluded. Looked me in the eye,
her head cocked sidewise. Shrugged.
Busied herself, without urgency, for the invisible cause
of other distractions.

Today in my reflection, I appraise
these swollen jowls, sagging brow,
a man rich with regret. Astounded by the possibilities,
to live again that brief run of luck, that lost moment
I lacked the courage to reach out
when the future might have twisted, reinvented itself,
with her small hand in mine.

Digging Deep

If you patrolled alleys when you were a kid
and dumped enough trashcans, sooner or later
you'd find something to carry home, something worth
tearing apart. Clocks were best — double-bell
alarms. Maybe the glass was smashed
and the hands on the face twisted or missing,
but the works inside still swiveled and clicked

and kept time. You could watch for hours, the tines
of one gear exactly meshed with the teeth of another,
the next gear snapping a featherweight rocker arm
precisely, the rocker's hair-thin wire tension spring
bending and relaxing, tick-tocking all afternoon.

But . . . you couldn't resist, couldn't stop yourself
from digging deeper, unscrewing the little screws
to separate the housing, then pinching and lifting
the miniature motion-makers free, arranging them
on the table like a surgeon dissecting someone's brain.

Till you've gone beyond reassembling what's undone. A panic
you've repeated over the years, peering quizzically in the mirror
this very morning after quarreling last night with a loved one,
regretting the curious and persistent habit
of wrecking things because you won't leave well-enough alone.

Hoops

My big brother played hoops in the driveway,
shot buckets through long afternoons, alone,
fast-breaking around invisible guards, faking it
past pretend forwards, slam-dunking the ball
for another two points on the imagined scoreboard.

Warm days with windows open, I could hear him
commentating the game's progression, emulating famous
radio sportscasters. In the final seconds on the clock,
he'd imitate his fans' enthusiasm, a deafening roar
which sounded a lot like the ocean if I closed my eyes.

He'd blush and look away when he discovered
his siblings listening, and we'd teeter
on the edge of cruelty, poised to spoil his dream.
That's exactly what we did, too often, though
we prospered little joy to witness the entire arena
falling silent in his fancy. Like a soap bubble

collapsing in on itself, the world we all inhabited
lost luster. The game ended. The players
slunk away, confused, ashamed. The crowd filed out
to the parking lot and drove home disappointed.
A hush fell on the afternoon, thick and sticky.
Sparrows cheering from the cheap seats forgot to sing.

The Cowboy Jitterbug

Well . . . the bride chose me to dance, insisted
I dance. I said I'm not a dancer, said
please, no. I'm painfully self-conscious
on the dance floor, fearing
my lack of grace and practice.

The groom had been enrolled in my writing
classes, painfully self-conscious,
lacking grace and practice. We fished together
on weekends. He was a local boy,
proud to show me where the lunkers waited.

She boldly clamped my wrist and yanked
me onto the floor in front of the band, twirled me
in a cowboy jitterbug till I was dizzy and drenched
in nervous sweat. She was a local girl,
tossed me side to side like slinging hay bales.

I staggered, blushing, reeling out of step,
the bride schooling me, manhandling me
like a thick-headed oaf. As the groom stood witness,
mute, confounded. As she threw me into the unfamiliar.
Till I cowered, a chastened stripling.

She'd humbled me, indeed, just like that.

The Poem You Asked For

Put me in a poem, you said. Remember?
Wanted your footnote in history,
a modicum of fame, your envious friends
peering in at your face
aglow on the page.

How noble your countenance,
enraptured between phrases, posed
(a bit self-consciously) in the desk lamp's spotlight,
a little half-smile lifted into your best
meditative gaze, one hand pressed against your chest,
as if exalted poetics had stolen your breath.

Once you've been immortalized
(and picked apart in Miss Morehead's
honors lit, where someone speckled
a sneeze on you, and several slept, and one
drew lewd bodies twisting in your margins)
life on the shelf gets old, doesn't it?

. . . waking morning after morning alone,
squaring the corners of your stanzas again,
fluffing the title and tossing it back in place.

Cats

The lounging house cat naps
sixteen hours a day, two-thirds
of his life lost in dreamland.
And learning this startles me
awake: How much of who I am
goes dozing even now, eyes
glazed in the bone-numbing
boredom of waiting my turn
at a stoplight, standing in line
at the ticket counter, pacing
airport hallways, my flight
delayed?
        Be here, be now,
says the enlightened master.
But how? I'm in the netherworld
so often, or somewhere between. Yea,
though I walk through the incandescence
of pretend daylight, I've slipped again
into twilight senselessness,
my life on hold till it's time
to board. Then I'll march

one-third awake, two-thirds sleeping,
toward my assigned seat on the plane
where I'll nod off haplessly
— head curled to tail —
in this persistent dream.

Natural History

Young scholar leaving the Natural History Museum
steps into a sudden bluster of dust, a swirl
of dried leaves and curbside trash. Drops

her armload of file folders when she reaches
to save her hat, and a flurry of loose pages
scatter like a flock of white wings.

Boys across the street, passersby, rally and sprint
to help the girl chase after and gather
what can be caught, returning the salvage

soiled and creased. That's it; end of story — naturally
no single understanding is complete. These boys continue now
toward their college. The scholar un-rumples her work

and smooths it back into place. The impersonal
and insatiable wind goes howling. A few irretrievable
graphs and explanations have escaped.

Friends

You could say we were friends.
Sort of.

We talked in the gym, stalling
between sets.

Honked if one of us saw the other
while driving by.

Noticed his name in the newspaper,
his business doing well. I'd say,

Hey, saw your name in the news.
He'd nod.

Mostly, the gym. Once or twice
a week. Couple years' worth

of grunting. Toweling sweat
and laughing. Saying nothing,

though the brain can be fooled
when you're pumped enough,

contriving what's mumbled in passing
to mean important things.

Life and death, for instance. And death
is not what you'd expect.

Especially, a man who took pains
to stay fit.

Who rose early, daily
donned his running shoes.

Who, at mile marker five, slipped
on the ice. Hit his head.

Hey, I wished I could say,
saw your name in the news.

He'd smile like it was nothing.
He'd nod.

A Prayer

A doe grazes in the moonlight.
If I weren't standing at the window,
she'd be grazing without me. If she
weren't out there, I'd still be here

peering into an empty meadow. But now
the doe fills the meadow, fills me
with . . . well, I'll call it *prayer*.
It's a strong word, maybe too strong.

Now and again, the doe lifts her head,
ears like radar, listening. The pair
of us awash in dim blue of the moon.
Separate stars and so much dark.

Waiting in Line at McDonald's,
I Clearly Perceive the Need for Education Reform

Teenage boy at one table,
putting the moves on a teenage girl
at a table nearby:

My uncle gave me the Harry Potter movie
for Christmas, and I watched it
fifty-two times the same day.

The girl scowls without looking up
from her fries. And says,

There's not even that many hours in a day.

I know, he says, picking something
from his braces,

I had to stay up all night.

Goodbye to the Old Maid

Now that she's passed, we struggle, my wife and I, to grasp
the whole of what's gone. She'd slept with us for sixteen years
at the foot of the bed, curled nose to tail, paws
tucked beneath her, ears politely folded back.
An old maid of sorts, spayed,
never to know the joys of coupling.

Except for having witnessed, embarrassingly nearby,
the raw noisy fact of it, her mistress and master
now and again in the grips of such fits
an errant leg might fly out
from blanketed nowhere

and send her tumbling
off the edge,
falling to the floor.

Blind Ambition

Mark with an X
a particular summit on the map.
Strap your pack at the trailhead
and go, crunching boot heels, climbing
into the horizon's early glow.

Let's not ask why you need to get there.
And, when you arrive, sweat-sopped, panting . . .
it's only human to bask in the quaver
of blood-rush, muscle, bone.

Behold, if you can bear it,
far-off peaks and purple vistas
shimmering in the midday haze.
Clusters of X's to mark on the map,
a lifetime of excursions,
a galaxy of destinations.

Now, you make your way back down
same way you came,
no longer blinded with ambition,
and pause to apprehend
marvels you'd passed hurriedly, earlier.

An underground stream seeping through granite,
moist rock greening precarious gardens
of moss, thread-like runners and miniature fronds
clinging to decay . . . as the flow burbles
up from darkness, and sunlight sparks

ice blue tongues of flame.

Blacktail Deer Road

Never mind my knees burned, bone against bone,
after the first hard-earned hundred miles, pedaling
from early hint of sunrise till nearly dark,
parched and exhausted. Never mind
the grit in my teeth when dust devils rose
and tore through rolling hills of sage, blasting me
sideways. Never mind the late summer sun
blistering my shoulders and thighs, rivulets of sweat
pooling in my ears, my neck sticky with brine.

Middle of that first night,
I woke with a full moon, my tent aglow,
hips stiff against the rubble.
                              Struggled to unzip
my bedroll and step outside to pee. Stood marveling
at the stars. Felt strangely at home . . .
a gypsy, maybe, glimpsing the road continuously
unfolding. Couldn't have guessed the strain

and ecstasy next morning cresting Red Rock Pass . . .
how aspen groves fluttered goosebumps up my spine.
How, gleefully, ragged cinders spit beneath my tread.
Half way to Yellowstone, how I'd finally ditch
my head's constant jabber. How I'd muscle the crank
as if the bike were pedaling me. *Never mind,*

never mind, a breeze hushed across fractured canyon walls
as, in a distant meadow, a scatter of antelope
lifted their heads to look at me and wonder.

Mechanical Marvel

Stopped behind a long line of cars and trucks
while road crews clear a rockslide . . .

Turn off the engine. Sit and consider awhile
this old car, faithful mechanical marvel
having carried you uphill and down,
so many ruts, so many backroads, so many
hard-earned miles over so many seasons.

Battered, faded, bent at the fenders a bit
as you are, too. But your vitals, say the gauges on the dash,
persist in the zone where they should be.
The intricate guts still grinding fuel into motion.
At the heart, tappets still ticking, though under pressure
more so now than when you first drove it
off the sales lot. And, yes, less luster.

But lasting, lasting. And that's the point,
isn't it? To continue powering ahead,
steering around the next blind curve, still chasing
another far and fetching horizon.
                                        So let's
praise this weathered chassis, these somewhat rusted
bones, the low groan of bad knees and stiffened
suspension. Give yourself this idle hour to doze,
to savor well-deserved repose. Let your valves cool,
look around and assess the depth of your tread.
                                        Turn
the key again in the ignition when the flagger
signals the wait has ended. Give it a little gas,
wake the pistons, feel the crank rev. Your familiar touch
easing the worn gearshift. You're both
still road-worthy, both ready to engage the clutch and go.

Monarch Reserve: Rosario, Mexico

Forget the facts a moment and step aside
from the guide who's lecturing the group.
Sure, the numbers tell us how many butterflies,
how many miles, how much time. Our craniums
packed with charts and graphs,
tallies of lost habitat, proof of species decline.

Step aside, and hear the cello of wings
thrumming chilled mountain air abuzz
with butterflies swarming to blood command.
One lands on your denim sleeve, unfolding
his royal colors, opening to disclose intricacies
of his design. Telling you he's more than just another

pretty bug. His tribe huddled in this exact spot,
pine boughs strained to nearly breaking, countless turns
around the mother-star long before your own kind
invented these pretend comprehensions. *Wake up,*

he's telling you this by the way his wings breathe
sunlight, amidst the guide's droning dissertations, the group's
note-taking misplaced regard. *Pay attention,* he says,
the forest floor littered with his glittering brethren
expired. While a kaleidoscope of mating couples
conquer the act midair.

The Snail Trail

of dried silver spittle
glistens on a rock pathway
climbing the hillside
behind my house.

I've lunged forward
and sweat my chores
up and down that pathway
with armloads of whatever
projects compelled me.

But the snail spoor
moves in slow circles.
As if he's lost his compass.
Headed nowhere.

He belly-slides in the dark.
Everything delicious.
Each pebble. Every green blade.
Worth going over.

Wherever he's to be
is not far off. He's certain of that.
And confident
he'll discover
whatever he finds.

IV. Shine

Is what I say true? Say "yes" quickly,
if you know, if you've known it
from the beginning of the universe.

— Rumi

The Grandmothers

In Mexico, on the cobbles,
I stood aside
for the grandmothers
on their knees. Grandmothers
on their bloody knees,

bleeding their way forward
toward the shrine.
I stood aside
to let them pass,
these grey-haired ancient ones,
tiny as children
draped in shawls,
weathered hands mumbling
prayer beads and rosaries.

I stood aside. They passed by.
Brown cobbles behind them
stained crimson.
I went ahead with my day,
exploring, tasting, listening.
I went ahead with my life.

I went ahead with my life,
I thought, unchanged.
And yet I carried home
this moment with *las abuelas*
— their torn flesh —
especially the one who stumbled

and reached out for my ankles.
The one who held tight to my pants cuff
and looked up at me,
looked into me.
                    Those dark eyes,
like faraway stars,
kingdom come,
flaming.

Mule Turds

A wrangler's string of pack mules
has scattered mounds of turds
along these twisted miles of trail.

Piles of fresh hay-green poop,
each clump a playground now for clusters
of orange, lace-fragile butterflies.

Each mile another thousand wings
opening to gather sunlight
while supping mule-ass sap.

We knew monarchs and swallowtails
when we were children, chasing them
with nets, but called these particular flaming

fancy-dancers "angels." What was holy
or not was wholly unimportant. Someone
had named their breed long before, and we

spoke the label casually, with no more weight
than we might say "potato" or "petunia" —
though it seems a suitable tag all these years after.

Who but angels could love shit?
And aren't we all squeezed through the bowels
of this earth? We trudge

up the trail, switchback by switchback,
huffing through mule dung. Each turd
gleaming in the sun, vapors rising.

So Unexpected

After we'd petitioned for works of art
to prettify our hallways, the artists
nailed up an unpleasant
series of black-and-white poster-sized photos
of AIDS patients — dying strangers, emaciated,
bedeviled, diseased.

As I passed from office to conference room
and back,
         these withered specters
were reaching to touch me, urging me
to lift my downcast glance.

I'd hidden myself inside myself, my focus
on the floor tiles. And learned, step by step,
courage to halt,
          turn aside cowardice,
and face the insufferable miseries of my kin.

So unexpected, where once I trudged past
into my cave, like an ancient creature in retreat . . .
how the air I breathe

now fills me. To live with these men
side by side, their tissue-rag skin, bone-raw
elbows and knees. To daily acknowledge
this darkness
in the hallway widening my eyes.

Baseball Reggae

This much we know;
no Protestant has moved like this
since the flames stopped licking their ankles.
— Stephen Dunn

Three barefoot resort-staff island girls
offer dance lessons each morning,
shouldering a mega-watt boombox
on the beach, calling out to sunbathers

who doff them away ungraciously
till the three shrug and commence
a small celebration all their own,
trading new moves, high-fiving
each other's best improvisations.

I do — sure as seagulls fly — wish
my hips were hinged like that.
Wish my frame's sinew and sticks
were better connected to mesh
and join in the music's contagion.

Today they reggae in the sand
and sway, grinning a pantomimed
softball, in which the pitcher's windup
lobs an invisible throw, the batter
swings and never misses, the fielder
twirls and launches to snag whatever
imagined challenge comes her way.

This one's mine! I yell out, surprising
the three who laugh and applaud
as I ballet deep into pretend left-center,
leaping to nab a would-be homer.

It's the best dance lesson of my life.
To not care a crab's ass as to who's watching.
Remembering how to play. No one
arguing a disputed foul.
No one keeping score.

Auntie Doe-Doe

Auntie Doe-Doe, bless her bones
underground, consumed us kids in constant fear
she'd scoop us up in her big strong arms
and smother us to her bosom
if we passed her too near. For this
we secretly admired her, though we dare
never let on. Simply wasn't characteristic

for my siblings and I to press flesh
to flesh, let alone to be lifted mid-stride,
cuddled and smooched on. Doe-Doe
wasn't really one of us, our parents explained,
an in-law. And we could tell the truth of that
by the way she couldn't stop being contrary
amidst our kind who kept our hands
to ourselves and stood apart like strangers.

We could conclude, too, by her flame-red
head of electric frizz — tied like a gypsy
with a black bandana — she'd risen from some other
bloodline, a rosy-cheeked race of soft round people.
People with green eyes bright as insect wings.
People who laughed a lot and wore freckles,
freckles everywhere like a room of loud wallpaper.

People who accentuated voluptuousness
by wearing a dust of powdered sugar
on their baking smocks. People who,
when we couldn't escape them, left us
blushing with lingering sweetness. Left us
brushing their smudges off our t-shirts. Left us
filling again with our accustomed emptiness.
Left us breathless and wanting more.

The Optimizer

The surgeons removed Uncle Harry's legs mid-thigh.
'Cuz he smokes and drinks too much, Mom said.
Uncle Harry enjoyed resting in bed, wiggling his toes.
"Ghost limb" they call that. An amputee's brain
can refuse to believe a missing limb isn't still attached.

We'd stop by on our walks home from school.
He'd be stripped to his boxer shorts, torso
propped with pillows. *Hand me my teeth,*
he'd say, and we'd pass him the jar on the nightstand
where his choppers soaked in their soda bath.
So I can smile handsome and proper, he'd say.

When quizzed how his long lost legs
were still dancing: *How should I know,* he'd laugh,
I'm stumped! Same joke, over and over. Or
he'd wrinkle up a grin: *This Christmas buy me tap shoes.*

The old fart couldn't dance even when he had legs,
Mom scolded. That's what fascinated us,
why we opened his beers when he asked, why
we lit his fags. Nothing could cripple him,

and we learned by his sarcasm to optimize the ridiculous,
the hilariously ridiculous, which was mostly everything
at hand, or a short step aside,

                               even on a bad day
when his kidneys gave out. We'd pester him
maybe more than he could stand. *Watch it, Sonny,*
he'd growl, *I'll kick your nose bloody
and you won't even see it coming.*

Pedestrian

His posture, his gait — this man
at the crosswalk, setting out
in full display, traversing four lanes
stopped behind a red light.

                        This pedestrian
concocting a show of it for impatient eyes
(he's rightly guessed) witnessing

his chin angled skyward, stiffened spine,
gaze fixed toward glory . . . as if to preen
in glinting robes of golden velvet
regaled for coronation,
this formal and glamorous
crossing curb to curb.
                  As if
he might wish to dazzle the world, blind us
to his rumpled overcoat, grease-stained
cuffs, shoes lacking laces, feet lacking socks.

Jury Duty

It takes, they say, a village
to raise a child. An extravagance
of tax dollars few of us gladly afford.
Why should I pay for a neighbor kid's
schooling now that my own offspring
have grown and gone? So sayest
the butcher, the baker, the candlestick maker,
and I can't justifiably condemn them
for feeling a bit pinched and put-upon.

And damn, when the summons arrived,
I wasn't particularly whelmed with civic pride.
Suddenly there I sat, this grey winter day,
in the jury box, twelve of us called
to hear the plaintiff's complaint tussling
with the defendant's defenses. Simple matter:
Prosecution alleges a man has been nabbed
for drinking and driving, while the man's lawyers
are commissioned to dutifully deny the charge.

Still, amidst the boredom of scripted legalities
and tedious protocol, I began — despite myself —
to marvel at the process of due process,
how it takes a whole village to define
our revered rights and to mete out determinations
when we've done wrong. Takes a whole day of *All rise*
and *Please be seated.* A litany of *Do you solemnly swear*
and *I object* and *Your Honor, may we approach the bench.*

Takes the barkeep who served the drinks,
and a table of buddies who laughed and slapped
each other's back until the bottle was gone.
Takes two cops in a cruiser, a siren,
pulsing red and blue lights, a pair of handcuffs.
Takes a county detention center detective
and his technicians to videotape the accused,
nine steps forward — toe to heel — and the same steps back.

Takes a warrant, when a man refuses a breath test,
to hold said man and transport him to the county hospital
where a phlebotomist draws blood and a nurse
certifies it's done exactly as prescribed. Takes
a signed, dated, regulation seal on the glass vial.
Takes a state crime lab and forensic scientists
to quantify the sample, write reports. Takes
a court stenographer, a bailiff, and the testimony
of witnesses and various credentialed experts.

Takes all of this and comes down to the jury
when examinations and cross-examinations have rested.
Takes the jurors, twelve strangers, awkward hours
to sift through their notes and dig deep for nerve
enough to speak what must be said. Takes
a shameful shit-load of tax money, the price
of justice for one, in order that we may proceed
hoping, when it comes our turn, there'll be justice for all.

Kinship

New skiff of snow covers roads and lawns.
Full moon above the night's overcast.
I drive past neighbors — two older gents —
shoveling slush, their sidewalks scraped clean
so passersby won't slip and crack an elbow.
Both men, now paused for conversation, side by side,

each leaning on his shovel, one stomping his boots
and the other craning his neck aimlessly skyward.
One says something offhand and the other
adds a thought back, neither casting an eye
directly face to face, as their meanings rise
in huffs of breath and float off into the vast

and lonely black. They pass nothing of substance
between them, nothing said outright. They relish
a stolen moment like this, and dawdle
shoulder to shoulder like a team of unharnessed stock
put to pasture. This moment I too enjoy, nodding
with these men, wordlessly. As I tap my horn in passing.

Romance

He's just a kid, really, nearing the cusp
of manhood, when suddenly he's beaming
and tells us he's worked two summers
hanging drywall and saved up
to buy a car of his own, his first.

Says he and his girl — well, just a friend —
drove that car fresh off the sales lot
high up a twisting mountain pass,
just for the hell of it, just for the joy . . .

and parked at the summit
to watch summer thunderheads gather
and to sit snug while a tsunami of fog
washed across the windshield, and the rain
flashed and passed over.
      Leaving them
alone and breathless, holding hands
when the sky opened, stepping out
to appreciate what a car can look like
starlit,
   what a glorious sheen
even a used wreck can muster
when falling in love.

Old Dog

In people-years
she's sixteen, but in dog-years
much older, so old
she should be doddering cautiously
room to room, pushing a walker.

Lucky for her, she can't do the math.
In her bones she knows not to hunt
for cause to lunge and bark. She'd rather nap,
though in fitful moments of sleep
she's pawing the air for traction,
joyously harassing a squirrel she's never
forgotten. Awake, she watches
the stillness in the trees, reluctant
to believe that squirrel is long gone.

Some days she leaps and fails,
then gathers herself, stares upward
as if the furniture itself betrayed her.
Later, we'll discover her perched
exactly where she'd hoped to go.
She'll growl menacingly at a dried leaf
blowing across the lawn. It's not
a real squirrel, but the exercise
and its outcomes are much the same.

The Giant Octopus

An octopus
— almost entirely squishy soft tissue —
can squeeze into impossibly small spaces,
a factoid offered by the marine biologist
as an almost plausible explanation
how the coastal aquarium's favorite attraction
had slipped the bonds of its keepers.

Must have discovered how to nudge the lid
of its glass confinement
enough to probe one tentacle
for a determined toehold in open air.

Must have hid like a rumpled dishrag
in a dark corner
outside the night custodian's view.

Must have heard the ocean
in the drain pipe
and slithered through.

A story worth telling, says the marine biologist.
Funny, how people are so convincingly disappointed
the aquarium's only giant octopus
has gone AWOL, he says.

More curious still, is how this story
makes even grumpy people smile, something
in us cheering a desperate primitive instinct
doing as it must
to find its way home.

Slapping the Octopi

One Aegean morning
I rise early to explore the streets
in grey light as windows blink open,
as shopkeepers yawn,
greet one another,
look up and guess the sky's intention.

As fishermen reel nets and stow traps.
As the star-weary crew chugs into port,
home from white-capped horizons,
the night's catch unloaded on the docks,
restaurateurs appraising iced crates of sardines.

The waiter serves me Turkish coffee,
crusty bread and jam. I'm writing postcards.
Along the shoreline below,
one shirtless old man shoulders a burlap sack
toward a particular table-topped boulder
where he spills his labor's net worth
— three octopi —
lifting each in turn over his head

and slapping them like laundered shirts
— *thwack thwack* —
smacking the lifeless flesh
against the stone.

This is done, the waiter explains, to tenderize the tentacles
before slicing and sizzling ringlets
in minced garlic and oil.

Now the sun casts its first rays
on a stalwart matron who kneels
to scrub the cobbles.
Now the bells call . . .
and worshippers, arm-in-arm,
file past toward early mass.

I work at my postcards furiously,
like I'm slapping them against the rocks.
Believe this: The world reveals itself
exactly,
so miraculously
it can't be written down.

The Sow

The sow and her twin cubs made merry
with a plastic birdfeeder
— brimming with nuts and sunflower seeds —
I'd tacked onto the tall native spruce
high up
outside our kitchen window.

The cubs clambered in the branches,
swung like monkeys
till the feeder's bracket tore lose
in a hail of granola
on momma bear's happy tongue.

While my wife and I
peered safe between slats
in the blinds, like two kids
huddled at a knothole
in the park fence, sneaking

a free show. Now and again
exclaiming in whispers,
She's knocked over the birdbath! or
The cubs are chewing through the garden hose!
And within a half hour
they'd left us

with a full afternoon of trash
and damages to repair.
One of those moments
in a long marriage, when we're walking
still holding hands, and talk returns
to memories carved into us.

Like the sow's teeth marks in the deck rails.

Goodbye

This massive, venerable witness to history
now leans toward its inevitable fall. This pine,
centuries past, sprouted on a mountainside
while nomadic tribes filed by, trailing game.
And rose till its crown crested a wilderness horizon
by which trappers and settlers set a course
westward. Its bark outlasted crews blasting granite
for graders paving trucking lanes along the lakeshore.

How small these cataclysms
under the sun and moon cycling, as this tree branched
its tenacious reach skyward, and scratched a foothold
in carbon star-shine and decay.

How small am I on my commute
twice daily over three decades, speeding by
this landmark's decline. First, uppermost boughs
bereft of needles, then lower limbs rusted.
Now the whole of its majesty barren of green.

When I trace with my palms the trunk's enormity,
and crane my neck to follow its climb,
some being still breathes in this wood and touches me
back.
       Once, when my children were small, they perched
on these roots, dipping bare toes in the frothing creek.
Here the wind rocked lullabies. Raptors nested.
A host of fledglings learned to fly.

A Passing

A passing glacier carved these stone spires
and mounded these humpbacked foothills of scree.
Enough ice can chisel granite. *Think about it,*
Jeff says, shouting and breathless, couple switchbacks
above. I'm picking my way toward him
through boulders which must have shaken the horizon
wide-eyed when each great weight came crashing.

We are trekking, this indelible day, to the top
of our lives, though neither of us would have guessed
the downhill side could be waiting so nearby. Jeff,
it should be documented here, is the blossom of earth-blood
and star-shine. I am an equal marvel, so are all creatures,

even you.

Think about it. This planet, paradise born in a blast of hell-fire . . .
the two of us resting on a rock ledge, sharing
handfuls of walnuts and raisins, passing a canteen.
Clouds racing past so near we could almost hitch
a lift. Each of us en route to one summit or another.
The life-span of a gnat. Almost invisible. So small.

Genesis

In the beginning, at the kitchen table,
my three children with paper and crayons,
shoulders bent low and hands fisting
the task before them.

Lo, through the wide windows
the morning shone down upon artistic intentions,
and the sun's slant rays rained
a glittered drift of pine pollen, spray of stardust,
as pages transformed, filled

with trees of leafy green, turquoise lake and sky, purple-grey
cluster of clouds enshrouding the highest reaches
of a distant craggy range. Whole neighborhoods
begotten. Barns. Fenced acres of spotted cattle, grazing.

And birds everywhere. I could hear them sing
as I passed through the room on this day
of creation, pulled on my boots, opened the door,
to behold the vastness, the particulars, the swirl

and churn of genesis, circumstance and inspiration,
my children and their children and theirs awash
in the world's possible outcomes, joyously enraptured, laboring
to guide the butterfly — this one colored orange/yellow —

supping from a tall flower,
which hath blossomed bold and blood red.
That one. Corner of the garden.
Edge of the page. Right there.

In Praise of Creation

Beneath these wings, the rippled plains
undulate in light and shadow, ascending
toward rocky steppes and snowcapped summits,
evergreen slopes on the eastern front melding
mile by mile into the Great Basin's red-rock and sage.

How could I do less than stare and wonder?
This planet's flesh-lovely form. Wish my hands
could trace and caress these shapes like shoulders
and hips and thighs. Voluptuous joy:
a cross country flight, window seat view.
                              Or better still,
a coast to coast road trip, downshifting to strain and climb
twisting switchbacks, the spit and slip of the tires' grip.
The engine's drag easing down the divide's other side,
following a cloudburst, swollen streams, the river
leveling into the valley below.
                              Or to pedal the backroads,
crunching through loose gravel, sweating across terrain,
inhaling breezes perfumed with bloom and decay,
stopping to rest my pulse in the shade of generous green.

None of these will outlast memories of my barefoot youth,
wandering game trails, the day-star
gilding each rock and meadow, dirt squeezed
between my toes, birdsong whistling through my teeth,
and my small heart cradled in the arms of each new day.

This Grey Morning

This grey morning, traffic jammed,
wipers slapping constant cold rain,

I'm strangely calmed, sustained
to relive in wondrous reverie

a mountain meadow, years
and years back, beside a green-blue

glacial pool, where I'd unlaced
my boots at the pebbled shore,

dared myself to dive and swim
— in the melt of snows eons old —

to plunge and rise naked, numbed,
shocked alive, under the day-star

beaming, a doe and her twin fawns
grazing nearby, unhurried, unafraid.

Epilog: You Have Reached the Spiritual Concerns Hotline

You Have Reached the Spiritual Concerns Hotline

For dogma, doctrine, and theories of the afterlife:

> *Press One.*

To smite an enemy:

> *Press Two.*

For confessions and lamentations:

> *Press Three.*

To bargain your way out of pain:

> *Press Four.*

For forgiveness and assurances:

> *Please hang up and dial again.*

For answers regarding mysteries of the universe:

> *Please hang up and dial again.*

For questions regarding your soul:

> *Please scrawl illegibly and post in a self-addressed, stamped envelope.*

To speak with your maker:

> *Please hold.*

Lowell Jaeger (Montana Poet Laureate 2017-2019) is a graduate of the Iowa Writers' Workshop, winner of the Grolier Poetry Peace Prize, and recipient of fellowships from the National Endowment for the Arts and the Montana Arts Council. He has taught creative writing at Flathead Valley Community College (Kalispell, Montana) for the past 35 years, and he has also been self-employed for many years as a silversmith/goldsmith. In 2010, Jaeger was awarded the Montana Governor's Humanities Award for his work in promoting civil civic discourse.

Also by Lowell Jaeger:

Or Maybe I Drift Off Alone (Shabda Press, 2016)
Driving the Back Road Home (Shabda Press, 2015)
How Quickly What's Passing Goes Past (Grayson Books, 2013)
WE (Main Street Rag Publishing, 2010)
Suddenly Out of a Long Sleep (Arctos Press, 2009)
Hope Against Hope (Utah State University Press, 1990)
War On War (Utah State University Press, 1988)

Edited by Lowell Jaeger and Hannah Bissell:

Poems Across the Big Sky II (Many Voices Press, 2017)
New Poets of the American West (Many Voices Press, 2010)
Poems Across the Big Sky (Many Voices Press, 2007)